John Farman

THE SHORT AND
BLOODY
HISTORY
OF
PIRATES

Red Fox

A Red Fox Book

Published by Random House Children's Books
20 Vauxhall Bridge Road, London SW1V 2SA

A division of The Random House Group Ltd
London Melbourne Sydney Auckland
Johannesburg and agencies throughout the world

Copyright © John Farman 2000

1 3 5 7 9 10 8 6 4 2

First published in Great Britain by
Red Fox Children's Books 2000

Printed and bound in Great Britain by
The Guernsey Press Co. Ltd

Papers used by Random House Group Ltd are natural,
recyclable products made from wood grown in sustainable forests.
The manufacturing processes conform to the
environmental regulations of the country of origins.

The Random House Group Limited Reg. No. 954009

www.randomhouse.co.uk

ISBN 0 09 940709 4

CONTENTS

WHO AND WHAT AND WHERE WERE PIRATES?

That probably seems a silly question. Everyone knows what pirates were – nasty, rough men with big hats, parrots and wooden legs, who sailed about in fab ships with loads of masts and cannons, yelling uncouth oaths and plundering and killing everyone that got in their way. Sure enough, all that stuff's more or less true, but it's really only half the story.

It's true to say, there've been pirates almost as long as there've been boats – Greek ones, Chinese ones, Viking ones, Welsh ones, Roman ones (Pontius Pirate?), and, believe it or not, there are loads around today – nasty modern ones.

7

In fact wherever there's a long and lonely trade route and an undefended prey, you'll find men trying to rob it. But the pirates I'm going to concentrate on are those from the mid-seventeenth to the mid-eighteenth centuries – the golden age of piracy – the ones you see in all the movies (with big hats, parrots and wooden legs).

Before we start, I must tell you that there were several different types of pirate at the time, who went under different names. I'd better explain, otherwise it might all be a bit confusing.

Privateers

Privateers were just as naughty as other pirates but had a piece of paper called a commission (or licence) from their Admiralty Court, more or less saying that it was all right to do whatever they liked to an enemy ship (rob, murder etc.) at times of war. The government thought it was onto a winner as it was supposed to take the lion's share of the booty. But many privateers like the mighty Captain Morgan (page 79) used their pirate's 'licence' with gay abandon, often attacking anything that moved, enemy or otherwise and stashing most of their plunder before they got home. Many of the Caribbean islands gave out their own licences willy-nilly to any old pirate who came along, purely for a share of the loot. The most famous privateers were the slave king John Hawkins and, much earlier in the 1500s, Sir Francis Drake (Elizabeth I's chum).

Corsairs

Corsair was the Italian name for privateer but it later became the collective name for the infamous Barbary pirates who hailed from the coastal regions of North Africa - places like Algiers, Tunis and Tripoli. These scary seafarers terrorised the Mediterranean Sea, in oar-powered warships, usually on the say-so of their deeply religious leaders. Often what they stole was their country's or state's only source of income (bloomin' cheek, if you ask me).

Buccaneers

Buccaneers were the pirates, usually English, French or Dutch, who hunted in and out of the Caribbean islands and later tried to get commissions (like what the privateers had) to save their grimy necks when eventually brought to trial. Although ruthless and jolly mean, they hardly ever attacked shipping from their own country. They got their name, by the way, from the first buccaneers who were hunters in the woods and valleys of Hispaniola (now Haiti and the Dominican Republic), and who lived by cutting up pigs and cows into strips and smoking them. (Not like cigarettes – silly – but by hanging them up over a fire in a smokehouse – an ancient method of preserving meat.) This process was called *boucaner* and the boucaniers who did it were known for their disgusting smell and bedraggled, bloodstained appearance. Anyway, in

the 1620s all these boucaniers became a bit fed up with the smoked meat business and decided to move to the seaside, where they built a load of boats and formed a huge gang called 'the Brethren of the Coast' – in another word buccaneers – or pirates.

How Many?

Records seem to show that around 1720, bang in the middle of the period I'm covering, there were between 1,800 and 2,400 American and British pirates prowling the seas, and roughly 13,000 naval seamen sworn to catch them. There are few records to tell us about all the others, but it's more than fair to say that travelling by sea carried enormous risk to life and limb in those not really so far off days.

Most pirates were recruited from captured merchantmen. Usually after all the fuss surrounding the plunder and pillage had died down, the pirate's quartermaster would step forward and ask if there were any men who fancied serving under the black flag (there were many versions of the skull and cross bones).

JACK RACKHAM

THOMAS TEW

BLACKBEARD

BARTHOLOMEW ROBERTS

EDWARD ENGLAND

STEDE BONNET

Usually quite a few, seeing what a laugh the pirates seemed to be having compared to the drudgery they suffered (for piddling money), threw caution to the wind and joined them. Most pirates, by the way, were aged between 17 and 50, with the majority being in their mid-twenties to early thirties.

Not All Laughs

But being a pirate wasn't all plain sailing and it had more than its fair share of downsides, as you might imagine. My book will tell you all about them, but also be prepared for some hair-raising stories of dastardly piratical deeds guaranteed to make your blood run cold. So, heave-ho, me hearties, let's splice the mainbrace (whatever that means) and cast off.

ALL IN A DAY'S WORK

I expect you think that when pirates weren't robbing and murdering, they simply lazed around the decks, swigging rum, yo-ho-ho-ing and generally having a pretty fab time. Well, you'd be right in some ways. Pirates had far less to do than merchant seamen, mostly because they usually had over ten times the manpower.

Having said that, running a three-masted pirate boat of 300 tons or more, with enough sail to wrap up Big Ben and enough rope to tie up . . . lots of things, was no easy job, even if there were up to 200 of you. Old ships needed a lot of work to keep them sort of . . . shipshape.

Having said all that, pirates never really looked for hard work, and preferred to indulge in their naughty habit of nicking someone else's ship when theirs became a little, how shall we say, 'knackered'. Even so, a new ship would still have to be maintained if it was to compete on the high seas.

A ship, even in years gone by, was quite a complicated piece of kit to look after. These days everything's made of metal, fibre glass or plastic, so boats are relatively (and that's a huge relatively) maintenance free. But the old ships that sailed before people realised that metal could float were a complex web of wood, canvas, rope and brass, that required more than their fair share of looking after. Anyone who has had anything to do with wooden boats knows that you can't just build 'em, put 'em in the water and sail off into the sunset. No way.

Careening

Those old tubs needed tons of elbow grease, not only to keep them upright but to keep the hull (the bit in the water) as smooth as possible so that they could sail at least as fast as the boats they were trying to catch or the ones that were trying to catch them. This laborious process of cleaning and maintaining the hull was called careening and the pirates hated it. What with all the barnacles and seaweed that clung to their bottoms (the boats', not the pirates'), or the dreaded teredo worm which chomped its way merrily into the wooden planking, rendering it about as seaworthy as a second hand sieve, the massive vessels would have to be dragged aground every couple of months. The whole crew would then be expected to scrub, scrape, replace any rotten timbers, fill up the leaky gaps between the planks with oakum (rope smothered in tar) and then paint the whole thing with a mixture of tallow, oil and brimstone, before giving it a thick coat of wax or tar.

This was a filthy, horrid, but ever so necessary job which had to be carried out on remote beaches (pirates couldn't just pull into ports like anyone else) and often in tropical weather, hot enough to bake a turtle or rainy enough to drown one.

And Then . . .

See, I told you being a pirate wasn't all laughs. As if that wasn't enough, while they were ashore, the pirate crew would then be expected to gather wood and search for streams or springs to fill all the water barrels to the brim. Then it would be out with the guns and clubs to go hunting whatever walked, crawled, slithered or flew out in front of them. Often this would be quite easy as most of the islands that they stopped on were so remote that the poor beasts had never seen humans before and let the pirates walk right up to them without batting an eyelid – and that usually went for the natives as well! Well, some of the natives. The clever ones knew what the lads were up to and chased them off their islands with bows and arrows and poisoned darts from blow pipes. Sometimes the pirates they caught ended up as a somewhat salty stew for the whole village.

Carpenter Ahoy!

Above decks, work had to be done to mend any of the structure that had been damaged in the last few months at sea. Whenever pirates attacked another ship, especially if it was a naval vessel, one of the first things they looked for were craftsmen. Most valuable of all would be a ship's carpenter,

usually an ex-shipwright, who would come into his own after a battle, patching up holes in the hull, mending broken spars and fashioning wooden legs as replacements for the injured real ones that sometimes he would have had to cut off. Pirate ships could never have enough carpenters.

Surgeon Ahoy!

Another great prize would be a surgeon. The Royal Navy always had a surgeon aboard, and pirates were so jealous that they'd nick 'em if they got half a chance. Pirates, you see, were always suffering terrible injuries, either in fights amongst themselves, or when attacking other ships, or just from all the terrible things that can happen when you get a load of men on a relatively small boat – like tripping over the ship's cat.

Cooper Ahoy!

Everything that was to be consumed on a pirate boat, be it bully beef, hard tack, water, beer or stronger liquor, was kept in barrels so therefore the next most important person on board was the cooper or barrel maker. He would not only make new barrels but repair the old ones and be an expert in how things should be preserved.

Very often craftsmen on naval or merchant ships weren't too bothered about being captured. For a start the pay was much better amongst the pirates. A carpenter, for instance, on a normal ship, although being one of the highest paid members of the crew, would make less than a pound a week, and the cooper half that. The surgeon would also be amongst the higher paid and would generally be regarded by the captain as an equal. A cook, by the way, only received about 50p a week on a non-pirate ship (and this was mostly reflected in the quality of grub he prepared). Secondly, if ever a pirate ship was captured and the crew were sent to trial, these craftsmen usually got off scot-free as they'd been forced to join the boat. Obviously they didn't talk too much about the share of the loot they'd no doubt received.

Slaves Ahoy!

Talking of natives (which we weren't), pirates soon caught on to the idea that they could be captured and made to do most of the hard work aboard ship. This became so popular that the buccaneers even hunted down the slave ships which plied the seas between Africa and the British colonies in the West Indies and stole their cargoes. So much so that in 1724 a group of highly miffed merchants trading with Jamaica wrote to the Council of Trade and Plantations in London complaining bitterly that the pirates were causing 'the havoc and destruction of the ships employed in the negro trade on which the being of our Colonies chiefly depends'.

Stealing People for Profit

The whole slave trade started when the European explorers, particularly the Portuguese, while trekking through Africa realised that there were thousands of natives standing around who didn't seem to be doing anything. The lazy Portuguese had always been short of people to work their land, so these unscrupulous men rounded the natives up and sent them back home to Portugal or Brazil. By the sixteenth century, everyone, including America, was in on the act. Everyone except England, who, rather miffed, cried, 'Why can't we have a share of all this lucrative trade?' (Actually, English privateers had been supplying the American colonies for years, but that was unofficial.)

The English generally got what they wanted in those days (how things have changed) and by 1713 all the Spanish colonies were getting their slaves from the British South Sea Company who made vast profits out of the Africans' misery. By the end of the seventeenth century, the main customers for slaves were the English owners of those southern American plantations. The poor, innocent Africans were treated worse than dogs – branded, chained, beaten and raped at every opportunity.

Cut-Price Slaves

To give you some idea of the value of slaves (if you'd wanted to buy one in the shops), it was reported that, in the early seventeenth century, a fairly average slave could change hands for as little as the value of a humble onion. Mind you, for all I know, onions could have been very expensive, but you know what I'm saying.

Pirates' Slaves

It was said that one very good thing came about because of the democratic way that pirate ships were run – 'all for one and one for all' etc. Some of the stronger and braver slaves were actually promoted to being proper pirates with even a share in the profits. But it must also be said that generally pirates were as bad as anyone else when it came to ill-treating their black brothers. Often slaves who were on the run from the disgusting conditions of the West Indies plantations, would beg to come aboard, but would often be treated even worse by their new pirate bosses.

The End of Slavery

This disgusting trade in human misery ended first in Denmark in 1792. Britain followed in 1807 and America followed a year later. Brazil, to its shame, only finally gave up slavery in 1888.

Barbary Corsairs

If conditions were bad on normal pirate boats you should have seen life in the galleys of the Barbary Corsairs who caused such havoc on the southern coast of England in the 1620s. These terrifying pirates from the Barbary coast seaports of Tunis, Tripoli, Sallee and Algiers, were mostly interested in slaves and particularly the nice strong English ones. They'd been given authorisation from their leaders to attack anything Christian, so for years they terrorised English beaches and seaside towns, dragging people from their homes and taverns to crew their boats. They would sometimes capture whole fishing fleets and any merchant ship trying to leave the bigger ports like Falmouth and Plymouth. The authorities in England, at one point, even had to smother the Lizard light, the famous warning on the southern tip of England, because it was turning out to be more use to the blinking Barbary pirates than to our boys. They even reckoned that if it carried on, in a few years the King would have no sailors left.

At the height of their success, the Turkish pirates had at least 20,000 Christians, mostly English, in captivity enduring the most horrendous conditions imaginable.

The long, narrow Barbary pirate galleys had not nearly the amount of sails as the rest of the shipping and relied on banks of oars (fifty plus) to propel them along at speeds of up to five miles an hour, especially useful when overhauling an enemy ship becalmed by lack of wind.

In the sweltering, stinking galleys, the rowers would be chained naked to their benches, expected to row for up to twenty hours at a time and were thrashed mercilessly if they so much as slowed down, let alone collapsed.* For food they would be given either a thin gruel or rusks soaked in water or vinegar. When a galley slave died, as they eventually did, he'd be unceremoniously tossed over the side and a slightly fresher one brought in.

HAVEN'T THEY HEARD OF SAILS?

Many of the captives decided that Christianity wasn't worth all the trouble (can you blame them?) and turned Turk which, on the good side, gave them better conditions and more food but on the downside involved the cruellest cut of all – circumcision. And on the even downer side it meant that, if captured, they'd be just as likely to be strung up as their new shipmates.

And strung up they were. In 1725 the Barbary pirates were driven from British waters by naval patrols who captured and hanged most of them with great relish.

* *They had to keep up with the strict drumbeat.*

ROTTEN FOOD
FOR ROTTEN MEN . . .

Probably the very worst bit about being a pirate was the grub. It was usually as bad as it can get and far worse than your granny's cooking or even school dinners. The problem was always about keeping the food fresh. Instead of having fridges or freezers, pirates were forced to keep their supplies in damp, stinky, dusty, leaky holds, which made food go off as soon as they looked at it. If they wanted meat, they either had to salt it before they set off (salt meat's pretty disgusting anyway), smoke it, or, literally, walk it on board – baaing, oinking, clucking, mooing and whatever noise goats make. Needless to say, the smell of the animals' quarters was only matched by that of the pirates', who, just like the animals, were not known to wash that often (see 'dysentery' page 36).

Pirates could, of course, catch fish but, as you might have guessed, they were a lazy, impatient bunch and usually couldn't be bothered. (Well, they couldn't be bothered till they absolutely had to.) When a crew ran out of grub altogether, no creature – be it turtles (or their eggs), penguins, seals (apparently horrible), seagulls, rats, bats – even grommets (the pirate name for cabin boys) – was completely safe.

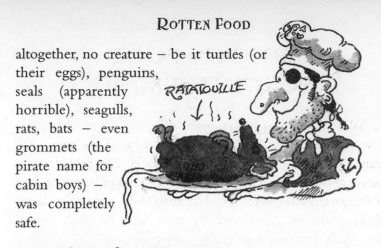

Eating ~~With~~ the Captain

To be fair, they probably didn't eat their cabin boys but it was not completely unknown for the starving crew to send someone down to the hold for one of the plumper slaves whom they'd stolen from some other ship or even captured themselves. Sorry, but I'm afraid I don't have a good recipe.

The motley crew of a ship that William Dampier (1624–1715), the explorer, was sailing with, were the worst rabble imaginable. They once secretly agreed, at a time when they were running a little short in the grub department, that the only thing for it, if the situation got much worse, was to dine on the captain and Dampier – as they were the only two worth eating.

By the Way

Chicken eggs were called cackle-fruit, for obvious reasons.

If pirates hadn't made their living robbing and murdering, they could have called in at all the big ports, like proper sailors, but because they were likely to get their necks well-stretched if they so much as tiptoed up the beach, they had to stay away. The only fresh supplies, therefore, had to be stolen from other ships or fishing boats, or plundered from small seaside villages, or simply hunted for when ashore.

Anyone for Lime Juice?

Because of their severe lack of vitamin C, due to their dreadful diet (no vegetables or fruit), pirates suffered from a horrid disease called scurvy (see page 33). In 1753 it was discovered that citrus fruits, particularly limes, did a lot to prevent this disease and from then on they always carried as many as possible on board.

Hard Tack

When everything else ran out the poor old pirates resorted to hard-tack, a sort of indigestible biscuit (certainly not chocolate Hobnobs) made simply from flour and water. After

a few weeks at sea, these biscuits were usually infested with big-headed weevil maggots who flourished in the damp, gloomy atmosphere – so much so that the starving men preferred to eat them in the dark. Weevils should definitely be not seen and not heard.

Pirate Recipes

The crew of the seventeenth century Welsh buccaneer, Sir Henry Morgan (see page 79) became so hungry on one of their longer voyages that they resorted to this rather gruesome recipe:

- Take one leather satchel (or indeed anything leathery – shoes, saddles, harnesses, Filofaxes etc.).

- Tenderise by rubbing the large pieces between heavy stones.
- Scrape off the hair from the rough side with a sharp knife.
- Cut into very small bite size pieces and add anything you have left for flavouring.
- Add salt and pepper to taste.
- Roast or boil till soft.
- Serve hot to starving crew.

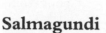

Salmagundi

When food was more plentiful, the pirates (especially Blackbeard) had a favourite dish which they always asked for in pirate restaurants. It was called salmagundi. Here's the recipe, should you ever have a buccaneer to breakfast, brunch or supper:

- Take some or all of the following ... turtle-meat, fish, pork, chicken, corned beef, ham, duck or pigeon.
- Chop into chunks and roast with cabbage (optional), anchovies, herring, mangoes, hard-boiled eggs, palm hearts, onions, olives, grapes and anything pickled.
- Chuck in – sorry – add, loads of garlic, salt, pepper and mustard seeds.
- Smother in oil and vinegar.
- Serve with as much rum or beer as your guest can get down his neck.

Indian Takeaway?

I'm not too sure whether this little incident should go in this section, but it is loosely to do with eating, so I'll press on. Christopher Condent, an English sailor and latter-day pirate, was a quartermaster on a New York merchant sloop. An

Indian seaman, fed up with being bullied by the rest of the crew, decided to blow up the ship for revenge (as you do). He was just about to light the pile of gunpowder he'd collected, when Condent – cutlass in one hand and pistol in the other – leapt down into the hold. The Indian, quick as a flash, grabbed another pistol and shot him, splintering his cutlass arm, but was hit in the middle of the head by the only shot that Condent managed to fire off.

The crew were understandably miffed with the Indian and, as the story goes, 'hack'd him to Pieces, and the Gunner ripped up his Belly, tore out his Heart, boiled it and eat it'. What the poor soul's heart was doing in his belly we'll never know – or the recipe he used – but I'm pretty sure you won't find it in any of your mum's books on Indian cooking (or cooking Indians).

HE'S TOUGHER, THAN WE THOUGHT"

And Drinks . . .

I bet you could have sold pirates any number of devices which supposedly converted seawater to fresh. Fresh water was a continual headache on pirate ships (or any ships come to that) as it was always stored in dirty old barrels and soon went putrid. Therefore, they took with them as many barrels of beer, wine, brandy and rum (grog*) as they could carry, and when they ran out of their own they would try their level best to pinch it off the ships they overran. And that, dear reader, is one of the main reasons why pirates were nearly always drunk.

* *Grog, by the way, was watered down rum.*

Bumboo

Perhaps the favourite drink of all pirates was called bumboo, a mixture of rum and sugar, flavoured with nutmeg.

Don't Try This at Home

On the downside, pirates sometimes had to resort to far less attractive drinks. On one occasion, pirate captain Bartholomew Roberts (1682-1722) and his crew of 124 men found themselves short yet again, with only sixty-three gallons of water to cross the Atlantic Ocean with. Due to poor winds, the days dragged into weeks and the weeks months, and the men, driven almost insane with thirst, were down to one mouthful of water a day. In the end they resorted to drinking seawater or, even worse, their own p— urine. Many died, but the ones who survived best were those who stuck to their rations. There's a lesson in that somewhere. However thirsty you are, don't ever be tempted to drink your own . . . well you know what I mean.

OPTIONAL EXTRA

HANDY HOOK

ESSENTIAL CARTOON PIRATEWEAR

BIG HATS AND BAGGY TROUSERS

Most guys (and girls) think that the sort of stuff they see pirates wearing in the movies is absolutely brilliant – big hats, baggy trousers, patches etc., but the bold buccaneers weren't really as flash as they appeared clothes-wise. Part of the job, you must realise, involved living in an atmosphere that was sometimes damp, sometimes windy, sometimes freezing and sometimes blisteringly hot. Not only that but they were constantly being doused in salt water. All of these things, plus the odd bullet hole or cutlass slash, have a tendency to make your clothes wear out real quick. Most times, however, they simply rotted off the bold buccaneers' backs.

GOSH- A BARE BUCCANEER

This, as you might imagine, was a bit of a headache for your average pirate because they usually only possessed the clothes they stood up in. Therefore, next to a good supply of grog and a worthwhile haul of trinkets every now and again, clothes, which were very expensive before the nineteenth century (mass manufacture and all that), became extremely precious.

What Shall I Wear Today?

Not a common question below decks. All seamen from the 1500s who *weren't* in the proper navy wore the same sort of kit – baggy canvas trousers called 'sloppers' cut off halfway down the calf (often made from worn out sails), a bright neckerchief (sometimes worn round the head) and a heavy loose-fitting woollen shirt belted at the waist. Pirates often plastered their clothes with black tar (hence, presumably, the nickname 'tars') to preserve them from the elephants – whoops – elements. This, as you can imagine, made them smell and feel ghastly. Worse still, pirates wore no pants or vests and only occasionally washed their clothes in sea water, so you can imagine just how smelly and itchy they became after only a couple of weeks at sea.

By the Way

I bet you can't guess why pirates nearly always wore a large golden earring. It was so that if they ever got washed up drowned after a shipwreck, there'd be enough money to give them a decent burial.

Shoe Free Zone

Ordinary pirates didn't generally go in for shoes, firstly because they couldn't usually afford them, having spent all their money on booze and gambling, and secondly, because bare feet gave better grip on a deck covered in water (or – on a good day – blood), and were more practical for shinning up ropes, monkey fashion. Also, it must be said, the pirates did occasionally eat them if they became really desperate (for recipe see page 22).

In the Mediterranean, where it got very hot, it was not unusual for the pirate crew to dispense with clothes altogether and swing about the rigging stark naked (allowing everything else to swing in the breeze, if you get my meaning).

Time to Dress Up

When the pirate captains, surgeons or quartermasters went ashore, they generally donned a kind of long, knee-length, brass-buttoned tunic which they belted round the waist over long stockings or even tights. On their heads would be the famous tricorn hat and on their feet the highly fashionable, large-buckled, tallish-heeled shoes or boots.

During the sixteenth century, sailors went in for huge baggy trousers called sloppes which only joined together below the knee. When they went ashore they simply wore a tunic over them, or tucked into their sloppes like a shirt.

In those days the captains often didn't look much smarter than anyone else when aboard ship, but whenever they went anywhere remotely special they dressed up to look like gentry, so's everyone would know who they were dealing with. Most pirate captains insisted on wearing these magnificent clothes when they went into battle and some even put them on when they were about to be hanged.

Ruff Trade

In the time of Sir Francis Drake (1540-1596) or Sir Walter Raleigh (1554-1618) a captain (even a pirate captain) would wear clothes consisting of breeches tied with coloured ribbons round the knees, a padded doublet, heavily embroidered and with a scattering of jewels, one of those soppy ruffs round the neck, a voluminous cloak, and all of this finished off with a cocked hat with a big, brightly coloured feather sticking out of it.

Just about everyone in those days had a beard and moustache (even some of the women, I wouldn't mind betting) and the ordinary sailors would have their hair scraped back to keep it out of their eyes and plaited into a tarry pigtail. Pirates seldom cut their hair and were only forced to do so when it became inhabited by stowaway lice.

Seventeenth Century Pirate Wear

They still had the same baggy trousers down to just below the knee, but this time with woollen stockings and a long shirt or coat. It was during this period that the extremely sissy-looking petticoat trousers became all the rage, especially with the captains. These looked a bit like long, knee-length, wide-at-the-bottom, divided skirts. The reason you don't see any of these outfits in pirate films is most likely because the directors don't want their heroes (or villains come to that) looking too soppy.

DAMMIT! I'VE LADDERED ME TIGHTS!

Cross-Dressing?

Talking of looking soppy, it was well recorded that when the rough and ragged pirates attacked a ship with ladies aboard, before doing anything else, they would rip off the poor damsels' clothes. Not, I must stress, to ogle at their naked bodies, or even to have their wicked way with them (that wasn't allowed) – but to nick their frocks. It was not that unusual to see a filthy, long-haired, tattooed, fully-armed, dead macho pirate leaping round the deck wearing the latest in seventeenth century high-court ladies' fashions.

SICK AS A PARROT

One of the main problems with being on a relatively small ship in a relatively huge ocean with a relatively unruly bunch of shipmates who not only didn't wash properly, but didn't eat or drink properly either, was that your bold buccaneer tended to be liable for just about every nasty disease going. Not only that, but a lot of seamen picked up some very unpleasant things from the lurid ports visited on their travels.

WHO ARE YOU CALLING AN UNPLEASANT THING

And it wouldn't be down to the sickroom, where a nice nurse would tend to their every need – oh no! If your average pirate woke up feeling a little under the weather there was a strong chance that he'd end up going over the side as fish food, for there was no such thing as a doctor aboard a pirate

ship (unless they'd captured one) let alone a nurse, and little in the way of medicine.

Sickness-wise, some places were worse than others. The pirates who hung around Europe and the cooler areas weren't at half the risk of those who sailed the 'Torrid Zones' – those seas round the scorching, mosquito-infested coasts of Africa. Just as an example, seamen on the slave ships that plied the waters between Africa and the West Indies, threw the corpses of four to five slaves overboard daily, as well as a fair proportion of their mates. It was much the same on the pirate ships. By the time a voyage was over, it was not unheard of for your average hardworking pirate to lose up to 40% of his chums.

So what were the main diseases?

Scurvy

Scurvy and sea-faring men go together like dogs and fleas. This disease is reckoned to have put paid to 200,000 seamen between 1500 and 1900. The problem was dietary. Sailors didn't seem to realise that a human being needs fruit and vegetables to keep reasonably healthy. Even if they had realised it, however, in those days on board ship there was no way of keeping produce from going rotten after more than a couple of days (see page 20).

When your mum and dad tell you that you must eat your greens they're not kidding (they're probably not pirates either, but we won't go into that). Scurvy is a nasty disease which results from a diet that includes no fruit or vegetables and therefore no vitamin C.

Symptoms
Loss of appetite, pale skin with dark blotches, spongy pimply gums which bleed easily, teeth falling out, swelling of the legs,

roughness of the skin, diarrhoea (even more unpleasant on a small ship with no lavs), awful lethargy and a certain loss of vision. If you happen to have all these symptoms, might I suggest you go straightaway to your local store and buy a load of sour lemons, limes or oranges and suck 'em dry. It has been said that the symptoms will miraculously clear up in a couple of days – mine did!

Interesting Fact?
British sailors were called 'limeys' because, after 1795, our Navy provided fresh lime juice on all voyages. The merchant navy followed in 1854.

Yellow Fever
One of the bad things about living in and around a hot sunny climate like you get in Africa and the Caribbean, is that you are far more likely to catch a horrid and scary disease called yellow fever which you really can live without, believe me. It was first 'discovered' by the infamous sixteenth century Spanish conquistadors when they conquered South America, and many say it served them damn well right. You can lay the blame for us humans catching yellow fever fairly and squarely at the feet (all six of 'em) of your common or garden mosquito and the forest monkeys from whom the mozzie picks up the disease.

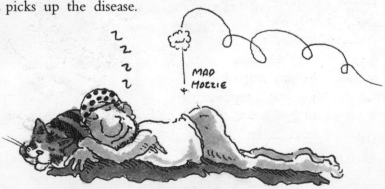

MAD MOZZIE

These days you'd be inoculated against it, but that sort of thing didn't exist around the seventeenth century so if, in the middle of the night, your potential target pirate was to have a visit, there was a fair chance that, providing the little varmint was carrying the disease, he'd get the full works. Which were:

Symptoms

For the first few days after being bitten, the patient could take it easy while the virus spread and multiplied throughout his body (yukk!). Then, suddenly, he'd get a chronic headache, backache, start being sick everywhere, and then he'd get hotter, and hotter and HOTTER. After three long, sweat-pouring, hallucinating days of utter unpleasantness, his fever would go either of two ways. It could be:

Good News: The patient would start to recover fully and, even better, be immune from yellow fever for the rest of his life.
OR

Bad News: He'd get progressively worse for three days, until he vomited black blood (urghh!) and then there wouldn't be any rest of his life. Mind you, I suppose it wasn't all bad news; after all, he couldn't get the disease again either, could he?

Dysentery (the bloody flux)

Dysentery is a very nasty business indeed and almost too yukky to talk about. You get it when a lot of people are crowded together, don't wash their hands after going to the toilet and then handle food. On a pirate ship, not only did they not have proper toilets (with soap dispensers and hand basins etc.), but the water was far too precious to be used for washing. Actually pirates were a filthy bunch who wouldn't have washed their hands anyway.

Symptoms

Don't worry, you'll soon know if you've got it: severe bouts of bloody diarrhoea, followed by severe stomach pains, followed by a severe thirst, followed, if you're a bit unlucky, by severe death. Severely not to be recommended.

Medical Tip

If you've got dysentery, don't, for God's sake, confuse it with scurvy for, if you rush for the fruit bowl, it'll more than likely make it much worse.

Psittacosis (Parrot Disease)

Talk about 'sick as a parrot'. This is where the term comes from. Psittacosis is a nasty little disease of birds (particularly parrots), which is easily transmitted to humans (particularly pirates). The joke is that the birds don't have that much of a bad time with the disease but humans get it much worse (if you call dying much worse).

SICK PARROT

How to Catch it
Easy! Go to your parrot's cage, put your head through the door (as you do) and sniff the bottom (of the cage, not the parrot). Psittacosis is caught from inhaling the dust of dried-out parrot poo.

Symptoms
The patient starts climbing on people's shoulders, flapping his arms about and copying everything they say at the top of his voice. Actually, that's a lie – it's worse than that. Someone with psittacosis suffers from a dreadfully high temperature of a hundred and something, followed by pneumonia, severe weakness and really fast breathing. It lasts two to three weeks after which time he either gets better . . . or he doesn't!

By the Way
Pirates really did have parrots as pets, not always because they wanted them, but because the pesky peckers would often follow the pirate ships when they left their desert islands thinking there'd be more to eat. Often they'd be lucky if the pirates didn't eat them.

Injury Time
These days, if we hurt ourselves, we either search for a plaster, swallow an antibiotic or, if it's something more serious, call an ambulance and rush forthwith to the nearest hospital where a fully trained staff will most-times sort us out (if you don't mind waiting). In the seventeenth century there were no such things as hospitals, proper surgeons or drugs like antibiotics to combat infection, and that was on land! Ships, and especially pirate ships, were much, much worse, and so were the sort of injuries you were likely to suffer. I mean, when did you last get hit on the back of the

head by a cannon ball or have your arm lopped
off by a cutlass?

Admittedly, on board ship one of the crew would usually
be delegated to tend to the injured. But his equipment would
be primitive, to say the least, and although he'd more than
likely have his own sharp knives (essential pirate kit), for
major operations like amputations he'd simply borrow a saw
off the ship's carpenter — if indeed he wasn't the ship's
carpenter.

Anaesthetic? Forget it. The patient would probably be
filled up with rum or brandy until sloshed to the point of
oblivion. This same alcohol would then be poured on the
open wound in a vain effort to ward off the horrid festering,
but often with little effect. One of the only ways of being sure
of stopping the infection was to put a lighted ember or red
hot iron to the injury (this was called cauterising) but the
patient had a nasty habit of dying from the treatment, which
was rather counterproductive. There is
absolutely no doubt that most of
the seamen who underwent
any form of surgery on pirate
ships would have died from
either the shock or the
infection that followed.
In fact those guys
hobbling around on wooden
legs could be regarded as
the lucky ones.

THAT'S REALLY
LUCKY

Gangrene

Gangrene not only sounds disgusting, but is! It's a horrible disease which results from the infection which sets in after a severe wound or burn. This would have been the usual cause of death to most pirates after a battle at sea. The flesh actually begins to rot you see (especially in hot weather), owing to a lack of blood supply. The smell, as you can imagine . . . is – er – unimaginable. The only thing you can do is to keep cutting back behind the gangrene in the hope that the wound won't re-infect, but you can end up with no limb at all – which is a bit tricky if you're a pirate.

An Eye for an Eye

Pirates were very aware of the dangers of so much fighting and a proportion of any stolen haul was set aside by the quartermaster to compensate the men for any serious injury received in battle. It went like this:

- Worst of all was the loss of a right arm – the cutlass arm. For that, if he survived, he could expect 600 pieces of eight (Spanish dollars).
- The other arm or either leg came in slightly less at 500 pieces.
- A lost eye was worth 100 pieces of eight (which would buy a lot of black patches) but I suppose it's fair to surmise the loss of both would have been considerably more than double. Let's face it, there are better things to be than a pirate if you can't see.

Malaria

Anyone or anything can and could catch malaria – birds, monkeys, lizards, corgis, hamsters, pirates – and, of course, us. Just like yellow fever, it is carried by mosquitoes, but this time, there's sixty different types of the little perishers to choose from. Four of these affect humans: *Plasmodium vivax*, which causes the sufferer to have a fever every other day (only half as bad); *Plasmodium malariae* which takes ages to appear and causes fever every three days (only a third as bad); and the last two, *Plasmodium ovale* which is quite mild and *Plasmodium falciparum* which gives you 'Jungle Fever' and causes coma and madness and kills you pretty quick by blocking the blood vessels to the brain (not that pirates had much brain to run blood vessels to).

Cure?

Ah, here lies the problem. Malaria is usually treated with quinine, a drug obtained from the bark of the cinchona tree, which is fine except it only grows in the Andean highlands of Peru – a slight problem if you're stuck in a boat miles from anywhere.

Consumption (Tuberculosis)

Very popular amongst those who live and work in cold, damp conditions with very poor food (in other words – pirate ships). A tricky little disease this, cos it has a nasty habit of lying around in the body for as long as it feels like before it decides to zap you. In fact a quarter of us have the bacillus *Mycobacterium tuberculosis* lurking around inside us without our ever knowing.

Symptoms

Obviously, this horrid disease shows no symptoms in the early stages (otherwise you'd know you had it), but after a while the patient starts feeling tired, feverish, loses his appetite and begins to lose weight. Then, if it's the worse kind, he starts having chest pains, coughs up blood and if he doesn't get taken immediately to hospital (which again is difficult if rocking about on the high seas) and isn't given a massive dose of antibiotics (not invented in those days), he usually dies – which most pirates had a habit of doing.

PUNISHING PIRATES

Almost all pirates had at one time or another been in the Navy or on merchant vessels – not by choice, but because they'd been 'pressed' into it. The press gang was feared by every hard drinking man in every tavern in every port in the world. When a captain was a bit short in the old crew department for a particular voyage, he'd send out a bunch of his roughest, toughest men, late in the evening, when he knew that most of the men in the taverns would be as drunk as parrots, and grab as many as he needed. By the time the poor souls sobered up, it would be too late, they'd be at sea and the only way back would be to swim (not much fun, let alone with a hangover . . .).

By the Way
When a man joined the Royal Navy in those days he'd receive a shilling from the King (rotten deal!). When a kidnapped seaman awoke aboard ship he would find a shilling 'pressed' in his hand. This was a cunning trick to prove he'd agreed willingly.

Once at sea, that's when the trouble started. Discipline on board for your average seaman would be cruel to the point of – er – ever so cruel. Disobedience could be punished in many ways. Sailors could be forced to swallow cockroaches, have their teeth knocked out, have iron bolts screwed into their mouths so's they'd choke on their own blood and, almost worst of all, be flogged by a frayed, tarred rope called a cat o'nine tails while tied to the main mast. Sometimes a man could be flogged over 500 times, and sometimes, just to add a little spice to the proceedings, the flogger would customise his whip by knotting the ends of the frayed bits or adding musket balls or even fish hooks (ouch!). Then, if the 'floggee' had been really naughty, they'd rub salt and vinegar into his raw flesh after the event – guaranteed to make the poor beggar's eyes water even more. I'll bet you never look at salt'n'vinegar crisps again!

Anyone for Keel Hauling?

Then there was always keel hauling, the horrendous punishment by which the guilty party was dragged under and across the bottom of the ship by a rope so that the barnacles scraped his skin off – a punishment that was often fatal, especially if the victim got a severe nibbling by sharks

All this for less than a quid a month – top whack – no thanks.

By the Way

In 1790 a lot of the worst punishments on British ships were banned when the *Articles of War* were published.

Pirate Punishments

You could still be punished on pirate ships but it generally wasn't quite so sadistic. Here are just a few examples:

Man Overboard

If a pirate was found guilty of a serious crime against another man, he'd either be chucked over the side and not thought of again, or towed behind the ship on a length of rope until he was either dead from hypothermia, exhaustion, boredom or simply drowning.

Marooning

If a crime wasn't quite so
bad, but naughty none
the less, the pirates
went in for
marooning – that
is, leaving the poor
bloke on some remote,
deserted island, or just a tiny raft,
with no provisions (unless you count
a gun to kill himself with if things started to look a bit too
tricky), and often no clothes. This was the punishment for
anything approaching mutiny or threatening the captain.

Dunking

At suppertime this was quite often done to the hard tack (see
page 22) to soften it, and slightly less often to pirates who
wouldn't do as they were told. They would lower the poor
blighter over and over into the ocean and, in between, hang
him up to dry in the blazing sun. Very good, as it happens, for
the old suntan but the victim very often ended up rather
overdone.

Rules is Rules

Everyone thinks that being a pirate for a living meant that you
didn't have to do all the stuff that proper sailors had to do –
wear proper uniforms, clean your teeth, obey orders, wash
every night, not answer back to the captain etc. But that was
sometimes far from the truth. As you might imagine, having
anything up to a couple of hundred rough, tough criminals on
one ship could create a few problems. Pirates often had a strict
set of rules to follow, and if they broke them, there'd be all hell
to pay.

Things Pirates Couldn't do

Oddly enough most pirate ships had a strict code of conduct, and this was often on display for all to see (and for all to sign). There were a few things that they just couldn't do — things like:

No Girls

Attempting to sneak women aboard, keeping them below decks or even disguising them as regular seamen were all forbidden. If pirates were found to be doing this, the punishment was short and swift. They were either flung over the side (often in shark infested waters), hung from the yard-arm, or simply run through by the captain's sword. Often pirates would be sailing for months or even years at a time. Because of the lack of women, many decided to cut their losses and find partners

CAUSE AND EFFECT

among themselves. Others waited till they hit the sea ports and often caught horrendous incurable diseases from the ladies of easy virtue.

It was forbidden to meddle with women of good birth from a captured ship. Penalty – DEATH. (It's usually thought that if pirates captured a ship, whatever was on board was theirs for the taking – including any women. Although they were generally allowed to have their will with the slaves and servant girls, they were strictly forbidden to ravage any of the posher women – probably because the captain wanted them for himself!)

No Stealing
Anyone who stole anything over the value of a piece of eight (there was no such thing as a piece of seven) would be marooned on a desert island.

No Secrets
If a man tried to keep a big secret from the other lads, he'd be sent away on a little raft with a small pistol, some powder, some shot, and a bottle of water if he was lucky.

No Violence
Any man who struck another on board and injured him could expect old Moses' eye-for-an-eye law – in this case thirty-nine lashes on his bare back.

No Dirt
If a man was found with a dirty weapon, and not ready at all times for service, or if he didn't do enough work around the place, he would forfeit his share of any stolen goods.

No Danger
If a man let off his musket for a laugh, or smoked his pipe down in the hold, or carried a candle without a cover, he got the same treatment as in the one before.

It Could Only Happen to Pirates (avoid this bit if you're at all squeamish)

After all that stuff about the sort of treatment that sent sailors to become pirates, you might want to hear of some of the things they did to others when *they* were calling the shots.

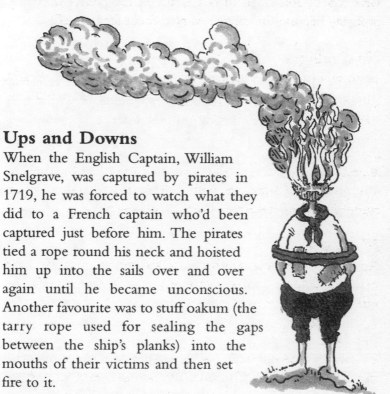

Ups and Downs

When the English Captain, William Snelgrave, was captured by pirates in 1719, he was forced to watch what they did to a French captain who'd been captured just before him. The pirates tied a rope round his neck and hoisted him up into the sails over and over again until he became unconscious. Another favourite was to stuff oakum (the tarry rope used for sealing the gaps between the ship's planks) into the mouths of their victims and then set fire to it.

No Sweat

A great pirate laugh was called 'sweating', a jolly little event in which the pirates would strip their victim and, to the tune of the ship's fiddler, force him to run round and round the mizzen mast by sticking him in the backside with knives, forks, harpoons or anything sharp they could get their hands

on – until he collapsed from exhaustion. If the pirates felt that wasn't enough, they sometimes put the exhausted man into a barrel full of cockroaches who would gorge themselves on his blood. Nice!

Musical Cannons

There's a picture in *'The Pirates'* by Douglas Botting of two pirates in the year 1718 careering round the deck on the backs of a couple of Portuguese monks, whipping their steeds until the loser's collapsed. Good game, as Brucie would say?

Woolding

You should have seen 'woolding' – the old pirate method of finding out where the valuables were hidden. This sounds pretty innocent – like something you do to sheep – but it involved tying the victim's arms and legs with rope and stretching him while at the same time beating him with all manner of implements. Then, just so's he didn't get too cosy, he would have burning matches inserted between his fingers, or slender cords twisted about his head until his eyes burst out of his skull. I did warn you!

Barbecue Time

Sir Henry Morgan (see page 79), who became the governor of Jamaica after a long career privateering, always made out he'd been rather nice to his prisoners. Oh yeah! Not according to reports of what he did to the women of Porto Bello when he captured the port in 1668. Apparently he threw them live on to a baking stove until well done, and all because he thought they had money, which of course they'd denied.

Blow Up

Then there were the buccaneers who tortured Dona Agustin de Rojas, probably the most important woman in Porto Bello. She was stripped naked and forced into an empty wine barrel. The barrel was then filled all round her with gunpowder and a pirate held a lighted taper, far too close for comfort, while demanding the whereabouts of her valuables.

Round the Mast

But that was nothing! French pirate chief Montbars of Languedoc had worked out a punishment all of his very own. Are you ready for this? He would slit open his victim's tummy and remove one end of his large intestine and nail it to a post. So far not so good. He would then force the poor blighter to dance round and round the post by beating him with a burning spar until his guts (all 25 feet of them) were played out and he expired. Phew!

Sorry, folks, but even I can't describe what Captain Morgan's men did to the Portuguese after capturing Gibraltar, but it made the things that I've already described seem like a trip round Disneyland.

LADIES AT SEA

Don't go thinking there were only men out there on the high seas. Okay, being a pirate was generally thought of as a man's job, but there were several well-known female buccanesses throughout history, which is all the more amazing as most of the time women weren't allowed anywhere near pirate ships (unless captives or slaves).

All the famous women pirates had originally crept on board dressed as boys and, strange as it may seem, managed to hide their gender from their macho shipmates for ages. This was even more difficult than you might imagine. All the guys on board the ships of the seventeenth and eighteenth centuries used to sleep together, eat together, go to the lav together, and, much more to the point, wash together – usually from a tub of water, and usually on deck in front of everyone. More crucial than that, as you can read in the chapter on clothes, in hot weather pirates would often charge around in their birthday suits.

Now it might have escaped your notice, but men and women have a habit of being slightly different physically. Couple that with having no Adam's apple, no five o'clock stubble, no hairy chest – not to mention a much higher voice and it all becomes mystifying, to say the very least, how the women were never spotted.

Here are a few lady pirates who not only got away with it, but were eventually able to 'come out' and be recognised for who they really were.

Anne Bonny

Anne Bonny was born in Ireland in the late seventeenth century, the illegitimate daughter of a well-known Cork lawyer named William Cormac. His wife kicked him out of the house when she discovered that he'd been having an affair with the maid (who ended up in prison on a false robbery charge). Little Anne was the result of their 'indiscretion'.

Now Cormac, as it happens, was very fond of his daughter, and decided that he'd like her to come and live with him, but he couldn't admit that she was actually his. He made out, therefore, that she was a boy and that he was simply training 'him' as a clerk. To cut the story short, it all got found out and Anne's dad, along with Anne and the maid (now out of jail), sailed to Carolina in America to start a new life.

But Anne became a bit of a wild child with a real sense of adventure and a talent for boxing, of all things. She got together with a young trainee pirate called James Bonny and together they sailed to the Bahamas to look for mischief. To cut the short story even shorter, she fell out with her husband and fell in with the swashbuckling 'Calico' Jack Rackham, a much hunted pirate captain, with whom she stole a ship and ran away to play proper pirates. But, as I said earlier, pirate ships didn't allow women, let alone wives, on board, so Anne simply reverted to what she knew best and became a chap again.

Mary Read

Mary Read was born in England around the end of the seventeenth century. Due to a little misunderstanding, her mother's husband had disappeared off to sea (before Mary was born) leaving Mary's mother with a young son. Her mother then became pregnant again almost immediately, by someone else (a real disgrace in those days) and, just before the baby (Mary) was born, the son died (so far so bad). Then, to avoid admitting to an illegitimate child and so as to get money off her runaway husband's rich parents, Mary's mother moved away and made out that Mary was the baby boy who had died. From then on, therefore, Mary had to be male. Clear so far?

At thirteen, Mary was found a job in a big London house as a footboy not a maid. But she found this boring and also ran away to sea like her mum's old husband, still dressed as a

lad. After this, she joined the army, but carelessly fell in love –
with a boy (there's always a catch somewhere), who, as you
might imagine, at
first thought it a
trifle odd, until
Mary revealed her true
identity.

OOC FUNNY BLOKE!

Anyway, they left the
army and started a pub
together, but hubby
carelessly died and, in
1697, Mary, who wasn't
really cut out for pub
life, put on men's clothes
once more, became a soldier again and was posted to the West
Indies. Guess what? The ship was captured by pirates and our
Mary found herself in the same crew with Rackham and the
other man/woman – the extremely butch Anne Bonny. Oh
dear, oh dear, Anne Bonny really fancied the dashing young
'man' and actually tried it on, to such a point that it became
necessary to 'compare notes', so to speak. Anne then confessed
all to her lover Calico Jack Rackham, who told them both,
for heaven's sake, to keep the fact that they were women
under their hats (and their shirts). But then Mary suddenly
fancied a fellow pirate and revealed all.

The two women, always dressed as men, were a formidable
team, however. And were every bit as fierce and fearless as the
rest of the crew. In 1720, after a short career of severe
swashbuckling, when anchored off the island of Jamaica,
Rackham and his merry men (and two women) were
suddenly attacked by a British naval sloop. Rackham and the
men were below decks lying around in a drunken stupor after
a heavy night, so the two women fought the Navy single

handed with pistols, cutlasses, axes and anything they could lay their hands on. They were magnificent. Eventually, however, when even *they* realised the game was up, they turned on their mates, who were now hiding below, calling them all cowards and killing and injuring several.

When Rackham and the rest of the crew were finally executed at St Jago de la Vega in Jamaica, Mary and Anne, also accused of 'Piracies, Felonies, and Robberies ... on the High Sea', were found guilty but got off on a technicality. While awaiting trial, they cleverly wheedled themselves into pregnancy and it was the rule in those days that pregnant women could not be hanged – neat eh!

By the Way
Just to prove what a toughie Anne Bonny was, when visiting her husband Calico Jack waiting for execution, she told him that she was admittedly sorry to see him in such a predicament, but that if he'd fought like a man, he wouldn't be about to be hanged like a dog (who hangs dogs anyway, I ask myself?).

And later?

Mary died shortly after, before the birth of her baby, having caught the dreaded yellow fever (see page 34) in jail. It was rumoured that Anne's wealthy dad (remember him?) bought his daughter's release.

Grace O'Malley

If you're one of those people who are interested in buried treasure and stuff like that, you might be interested in Grace O'Malley, the sixteenth century Irish piratess who apparently buried nine tons of it. But before you go out with your bucket and spade, beware . . . Old Grace apparently laid a nasty curse on anyone who should happen to find it. (Mean or what?)

Grace O'Malley came from the mighty and powerful O'Malley family who had forts and castles all over Belclare and on Clare Island on the west coast of Ireland, as well as a huge fleet of pirate ships. Grace, by the way, when a little girl, was horribly scarred on the face by the beak and talons of a naughty eagle, whom she was trying to dissuade from carrying off her daddy's lambs.

Anyway, Mr O'Malley trained his daughter to be a brave warrior(ess) and, when he died, she took over as leader of the terrifying O'Malley pirates, who caused havoc all along the coast of Ireland. So much so that Queen Elizabeth I offered £500 (around £75,000 in modern money) for her capture.

Grace really was some girl by all accounts, and there are hundreds of legends and stories about her bravery. Apparently, when a young mother (her son was one day old), she helped repel some Muslim pirates who were attacking her ship. Her captain supposedly came below to report that they were getting the worst of it. Grace cursed her crew and rushed on to the deck with a musket in one hand and presumably the nipper in the other shouting and screaming fit to frighten the very bravest Muslim.

Later, when sixty years old, she attacked a Spanish vessel just off the coast of Ireland, this time crashing on to the deck in her nightie, waving her pistols about and looking simply frightful in her curlers and all. The poor Spaniards thought our Grace was some sort of horrid spectre and surrendered without a shot being fired.

By the Way

As a caring parent, it must be said, the old girl left a lot to be desired. Legend has it that on one occasion her poor son fell overboard while they were on their way home to Clare Island after a few weeks' persistent pirating. He eventually struggled to the side of the boat and grabbed at it, but his

THANKS A LOT MUM

mum chopped off his hand, leaving him to die in the waves claiming (quite rightly, I suppose) that had he been a true O'Malley, he wouldn't have fallen over in the first place. A hard way to learn a lesson, I'd have thought!

She was eventually captured but, after an eighteen-month stretch in Limerick gaol, soon returned to her old tricks again. In the meantime her hubbie had died and in those days, a wife had no right to her old man's lands. She was alone and vulnerable but, instead of waiting to be attacked by her hostile neighbours, old Grace attacked them first. She was captured yet again and this time her whole fleet was confiscated. But Grace appealed to Queen Elizabeth as one woman to another, claiming she'd been forced into it (a bit of a porkie, admittedly). But Lizzie rather liked the eccentric old girl and ordered her captors to sort it all out, to give her a break, and to let her live the rest of her life (she was 70) in comfort and peace. The old lady died aged 73 in 1603 and one of her brave sons went on to be Viscount Mayo.

Mrs Cheng

To be honest there were a quite few girl/boys like the ones I've just mentioned, but for all out scale you couldn't really beat the infamous Chinese pirate chief Cheng I Sao. Mrs Cheng, as she was known, was a

yo Ho Ho

Chinese prostitute from Canton and the widow of Cheng I who'd controlled all the sea between Hong Kong and Vietnam. Between him and his good lady wife they ruled an army of the most bloodthirsty pirates that had ever sailed the seven seas.

Nothing was safe from Mr and Mrs Cheng and they even ran a protection racket for the smaller merchant ships which they couldn't be bothered to plunder, as well as all the little fishing vessels that operated in the same waters. They were forced to pay fees at a series of collection posts along the coast.

Mr Cheng died violently in 1807 and his wife promptly appointed Chang Pao, a brilliant buccaneer whom her husband had once captured and later adopted, to command what she called the Red Flag Fleet. She, like her dead husband, had an affair with him (yes, you read it right) and later married him. While Mrs Cheng remained the total boss, Chang became in charge of operations. Their house (or boat) rules were even stricter than those of the Caribbean pirates and went along these lines:

1) For disobeying orders or nicking any of the treasure before it was shared out, it was off with your head and no messing.

2) Desertion or absence without leave was met with a severe loss in the ear department (both were chopped off).

3) If plundered goods were concealed it was a whipping of the worst order, and on a second offence – it was severe head removal again (well not actually again, but you know what I mean).

4) Rape of women prisoners was punished by death, but if – and here's the rub – the woman in question had agreed to it, it was still off with the head for the bloke, and over the side for the woman (with a heavy weight tied to her ankles).

Mrs Cheng became so powerful that even the Chinese army and navy couldn't get near her. She had nearly four hundred ocean-going junks, larger than many a countrys' navy and at times up to 7,000 men. And, oh boy, was she cruel. At one time in 1809 her lads attacked a village that had helped her enemies, and took horrible revenge. They burned it to the ground and beheaded its eighty male inhabitants, hanging their heads on a large banyan tree as a warning to others. (Don't stand too close to banyan trees?) The women and children were dragged off to the boats to be done with as Mrs Cheng saw fit.

In the end the Chinese asked for the help of the British and Portuguese navies. But even that didn't work – the pirates were just too powerful. So the Chinese government offered Cheng and Chang an amnesty (basically if they promised to be good right away, they'd be free from prosecution).

Mrs Cheng and Chang Pao went for the idea, and settled down in Canton, where the former opened Cheng's Chinese takeaway – no she didn't, she opened a massive gambling house and died, aged sixty nine, an immensely rich old lady.

PIRATE FUN

Being a pirate wasn't all capturing treasure ships, swigging grog, counting treasure and stuff like that. Much of the time was spent lounging around on deck, either becalmed, or just desperate for something to come over the horizon that they could molest. Pirate ships, if you think about it, weren't often actually going anywhere, so they'd loiter around the trade routes waiting for ships that actually were. Sometimes they could hang about for months and therefore had to amuse themselves as best they could. Here are a few of the things they got up to:

Heads You Win

Pirates loved to gamble with cards, dice or even who they were going to capture next and gambling was almost as popular as drinking (well almost). One of the problems was that pirates being pirates, they could get completely carried away and lose all their property, not to mention the clothes they stood up in or even their wives back home. And, almost inevitably, just like in the cowboy films, it would all end in a massive fight. Many captains, like privateer Woodes Rogers actually had to ban gambling of any kind on board his ship, the *Duke*, and make everyone, right down to the cabin-boy's parrot, sign a document, in case they

PIRATE PANTS

changed their minds.

Some captains who didn't actually ban gambling were often able to use the sailors' inability to control their weakness to their advantage. You see, the trouble with big pirate ships (just like small kids), had always been that when the crew wanted to go ashore for fun and frolics, someone had to stay behind to look after it. Obviously all those who had lost their hard fought-for money had to stay aboard to look after the ship while the others hit the town.

Mock Trials

Most pirates, despite being a bloodthirsty lot, were pretty scared of the prospect of what would happen to them if they ever got nicked – a quickish trial, a tallish gibbet and a longish rope – if they were lucky! It became quite common to act out a mock trial, a weird kind of pantomime where everyone aboard dressed up for his part. The captain was usually the judge and the rest of the crew would play the lawyers, jury, jailer and, would you believe it, hangman. In this way they were able to make light of their almost inevitable fate – to spit in its face – so to speak.

These trials were often acted out with

DID ANYONE PACK THE SCRABBLE?

such reality that the poor accused (usually not the brightest member of the crew) became genuinely scared for his life. On one occasion in 1717, a young pirate got himself into such a tizz that he thought his fellow shipmates really were going to hang him. He lost the plot so badly, in fact, that he threw a home-made grenade at the mock jury and then drew his cutlass and hacked off the arm of the guy acting as the prosecuting lawyer – a pirate who went by the name of Alexander the Great (from then on presumably, Alexander the One-Armed Great).

Party Time

Every time pirates overhauled a ship they'd have a wild party when they got back to their own boat. As we've already established, they loved to booze and were crazy about drinking toasts to just about anyone they could think of – their wives, mistresses, friends, parrots, shipmates, past conquests, future conquests – you name it. Some of the most popular toasts were to God or the Devil, or death to any of a whole gaggle of judges, naval captains or even royalty who were after their greasy necks. It is said that on the pirate island of Madagascar in the Indian Ocean the speciality was to mix gunpowder with the rum for specially solemn oaths and toasts. Madagascar, by the way, was almost exclusively a pirate island from the 1680s right into the eighteenth century and many of the leaders had private armies surrounding their massive fortress-like houses.

There were, in fact, many pirate havens where like-minded villains could relax and party to their heart's content with their feet firmly on dry land. The pirates tended to favour tricky little harbours which huge men-of-war couldn't follow them into, and these were chosen by their nearness to the trade routes, and their far-awayness from the powers that were out to get them. Places like the French island of Tortuga, New Providence Island (now Nassau), the Juan Fernandez Islands near Chile, Devil's Island off Guiana, and Ocrakoke island on the North Carolina coast, to name a few. But their real favourites were the corrupt ports which operated outside the law and actually encouraged the pirates' lucrative business – Port Royal in Jamaica (the naughtiest city in the world), Algiers on the North African Coast, and Fort Dauphine on the aforementioned island of Madagascar for example.

Pirate Music

Music was essential to keep pirates' spirits up. Most naval and merchant captains would insist on a ship's band or even a small orchestra. There's no reason to suppose that pirate ships didn't do the same. We know, for instance, that one of the most prized treasures to be removed from a conquered ship (after the carpenter and surgeon) would be anyone who could play a musical instrument like a fiddle or squeeze-box.

These musicians often didn't mind being captured that much, as, without doubt, their duties on a pirate ship would be much lighter and, let's face it, being captured was an almost watertight defence if they ever came to trial.

Music While You Work

There would be music while the crew ate their supper, scrubbed the deck, spliced the mainbrace, shivered their timbers and most evenings before bedtime. And then there were the dances.

YOU DANCE DIVINELY

Pirates loved to dance and thought nothing of getting up and dancing with each other to the hornpipe or jig. Best of all, the ship's band would play rousing battle songs while the rest of the pirates were chasing and attacking other boats – banging drums and crashing cymbals and generally making a God-awful din simply to scare the wits out of their prospective victims.

(I'd just play a selection from *Cats*.)

Many of the pirates' shanties are far too rude for my publishers to allow and mostly boast about their exploits not only when fighting but with the opposite sex. Others were sad, whiney laments about their sweethearts back home or what was going to happen to them if they ever got nicked.

Here are a couple of examples of the more publishable ones:

Across the Ocean I Must Wander

Well it's all for me grog, me jolly, jolly grog,
It's all for me beer and tobacco,
For I spent all me tin on the lassies drinking gin,
Far across the ocean I must wander.

Where are me boots, me noggin', noggin', boots?
They're all gone for beer and tobacco,
For the heels they are worn and the toes kicked about
And the soles are looking for better weather.

Where is me shirt, me noggin', noggin' shirt,
It's all gone or beer and tobacco,
For the collar is all worn, and the sleeves they are all torn,
And the tail is looking out for better weather.

I'm sick in the head and I haven't been to bed,
Since I first came ashore for me slumber,
For I spent all me dough on the lassies don't you know,
Far across the western ocean I must wander.

Cheerily Man

O Nancy Dawson, Hio!
Cheer'ly man;
She's got a notion Hio-o!
Refrain:
Cheer'ly man;
For our old bo'sun, Hio!
Cheer'ly man, O!
Hauley, Hio-o!
Cheer'ly man.

O Betsey Baker, Hio!
Cheer'ly man;
Lived in Long Acre, Hio-o!
Cheer'ly man;
Married a Quaker. Hio!
Refrain:

O Sally Rackett, Hio!
Cheer'ly man;
Pawned my best jacket, Hio-o!
Cheer'ly man;
And kept the ticket. Hio!
Refrain:

O the ladies of town, Hio!
Cheer'ly man;
All soft as dawn, Hio-o!
Cheer'ly man;
In their best gown. Hio!
Refrain:

O Polly Hawkins, Hio!
Cheer'ly man;
With her white stockings, Hio!
Cheer'ly man;
Beats all at talking. Hio!
Refrain:

O Kitty Carson, Hio!
Cheer'ly man;
Jilted the parson, Hio-o!
Cheer'ly man;
Married a mason. Hio!
Refrain:

O haughty cocks, Hio!
Cheer'ly man;
O split the blocks, Hio-o!
Cheer'ly man;
O stretch her luff. Hio!
Refrain:

THE PICK OF THE BUNCH

There were thousands of pirates terrorising the seven seas during the seventeenth and eighteenth centuries, but some stood out head and shoulders above the rest. Here's the pick of the best – or worst – of 'em!

Blackbeard – The Weirdest

Blackbeard was the nickname given to a nasty piece of work called Edward Teach, who was born in Bristol sometime in the late seventeenth century. In a way he was a failed sailor who turned lawbreaker because he wasn't getting anywhere in the Navy. Nonetheless, he was to gain a reputation as one of the most terrifying of all pirates and is now more talked about than any of the famous proper naval captains of the day. Here are just a few of the stories about the old devil.

Appearance

Not content with being fierce, Blackbeard had to *look* fierce as well. He had a good start, for he was built like an all-in wrestler with a horribly twisted nose and big sticky-out ears. He added to this by sporting a huge, shaggy beard (black obviously) which he wore in filthy ringlets. To set all this off, Blackbeard would wear a black wide-brimmed pirate hat pulled down right to his eyes and, best of all, when in fighting mode, he would weave hemp cords soaked in saltpetre and limewater into his hair and beard and light them, so surrounding his massive head with an eerie glow and thick black smoke.

His demonic appearance was accompanied by a bandoleer with three braces of pistols ready for action and a wide belt with even more pistols and various nasty-looking daggers and cutlasses. Not someone you'd want to meet on a dark night in a small boat, I'll wager.

Fun and Games

In order to show his crew who was boss, Blackbeard would think up daft tests of bravery and endurance. Like creating a 'hell' of his very own, which he did by challenging his toughest sailors to accompany him down below, where he battened down all the hatches and lit pots of lethal brimstone. As the choking yellow fumes filled the pirates' parlour, one by one the crew dashed gasping in to the fresh air, while Blackbeard remained laughing fit to burst.

Gaining Respect

Another time, he was sitting at a table, down below, having a pleasant after-work drink with his mates, when he suddenly blew out the candles and pulled out his two huge pistols. Before anyone could get a word out, he shot right under the table, smashing the knee of Israel Hands, his second in command, who was taken immediately to the wooden leg department.

When the others rather falteringly asked why exactly he'd done it, Blackbeard replied quite calmly that if he didn't shoot one of his crew every now and again, they might forget exactly who he was – which is fair enough I suppose.

Nautical Naughties

Blackbeard had upwards of fourteen wives, all under twenty and a few hardly more than fifteen. Generous to a fault, he would share them with the rest of the crew.

Caution

Further research (like reading *The Wordsworth Dictionary of Pirates*) suggests that some of these stories are a trifle exaggerated – made up by the great novelist and historian (and fibber) Daniel Defoe (who'd say anything to flog a few more books). True, Edward Teach, alias Blackbeard, was very much on the wrong side of respectability, and true you wouldn't want him to marry your sister (or maybe you would!), but there is no proper, documented record of his ever really killing or torturing anyone for a laugh. As for all his sexual antics, indeed many historians now believe that he was actually afraid of women.

But, none the less, he did commit some gross acts of piracy, did cheat his crew out of most of their share of the bounty, and did manage to die in the most spectacular manner.

Blackbeard Backs Out – Ungracefully

On 17 November 1718, two naval sloops sailed south to capture Edward Teach who by now had £100 (and his famous wide brimmed hat) on his head. They caught up with his ship, the *Adventure*, five days later at the Ocrakoke inlet, North Carolina – the old blackguard's favourite hidey-hole. When Blackbeard realised who they were, he laughed heartily, downed a huge tankard of rum and yelled across to the officers on the other boat: 'Damnation to anyone who should give or ask quarter [mercy].' Which was a trifle rude, you must admit.

The young Lieutenant Maynard, who was in command of one of the naval sloops, shouted back, 'I shall expect no quarter from you and shall give none.' Fighting talk in anyone's language.

After a God-almighty scrap between the ships, the two captains finally came face to horrible face on Maynard's deck. (Blackbeard and his merry men had rudely boarded without so much as an invitation.) First it was pistols. Blackbeard's missed due to his inebriated state but Maynard's hit home, unfortunately having absolutely no effect whatsoever. Then, just like in the movies, it was cutlasses. They fought hard until poor Maynard's blade was broken in two. Then, just as Maynard stepped back to cock his other pistol, Blackbeard lumbered forward for the kill. Unfortunately (for Blackbeard), a naval seaman rather unsportingly jumped in his way and slashed him right across the throat as he passed, causing him to spout a frothy fountain of blood and generally make a terrible mess everywhere. The brave lieutenant, now ready, managed to shoot Blackbeard again but, once more, it didn't stop him. But another slash from a broadsword right across the back of his neck did. (I'm surprised his head didn't fall right off.) Well, it did stop him, but it still didn't bring him down. The old sea dog, bleeding and cursing like a good'un wavered for what seemed ages, trying desperately to cock another of his many pistols. Eventually, however, he crashed, like a bewildered bull in a bullring, to the blood-soaked deck – stone cold dead. When they finally examined his body they found twenty-five separate wounds.

All the other pirates, by the way, either surrendered or dived over the sides before you could say 'shiver my timbers'. They hadn't even waited to see the boss's huge head finally being severed from his huge body and stuck triumphantly on the front of Maynard's sloop as a grisly trophy.

Bartholomew Roberts – The Cleverest

Welshman Bartholemew Roberts, born in 1682, had been an honest hard-working seaman both in the Navy and on merchant ships for over thirty years. He was a natural sailor but realised, like Blackbeard, that his dream of becoming a captain was never going to happen – certainly not on the right side of the law.

His life of villainy started almost by accident. He was second mate on a slave ship called the *Princess* when it (and he) were captured by another Welshman, pirate captain Howel Davis in his ship the *Rover*. Now Davis actually liked Roberts but couldn't persuade him to join in the pirate fun. It was only when Davis was shot dead during a rather daring raid that the swarthy crew asked our Bartholomew if he'd like to be their captain (they hadn't a clue how to sail the damn boat). Blow this being a prisoner for a lark, he thought and decided to reject King and country and accept their

generous
offer.
Let's face it,
if you're
going to be a
pirate, you might as
well be the captain!

Bartholomew
Roberts or Black Bart
(as he was soon nicknamed)
was to become probably the
greatest pirate captain ever.
There was no more spectacular
mariner to be found in all the
seven seas, and no more
flamboyant, in his crimson
waistcoat and breeches, red
feather stuck in tricorn hat, his

BARTHOLOMEW ROBERTS

flash diamond cross on a thick gold chain and two pairs of
pistols hanging off a red silk sling over his shoulders – brilliant
stuff.

On his first trip he struck gold – literally – running into a
fleet of forty-two Portuguese ships parked (or should that be
moored) in the harbour of Bahia on the Brazilian coast,
waiting for an armed escort. The first boat they attacked
turned out to be the richest and Black Bart and his crew
escaped with a haul of 90,000 gold moidores and chests of
fabulous jewellery including that priceless diamond cross
specially made for the King of Portugal, which the pirate
captain was to wear at all times. Almost best of all were bales
of fine tobacco which, by the way, the pirates had just run out
of (there's nowhere to get fags on the high seas). Not a shot
had been fired.

Black Bart was an extraordinary bloke, being ever so cruel on the one hand but terribly fair on the other. His code of rules on board ship was designed so that each man should be treated equally and honestly – odd on a ship whose sole purpose was to rob and kill with maximum barbarity.

Bart's Rules (well some of them):

- All candles were to be out by eight o'clock – bedtime. Anyone who wanted to carry on drinking had to do it on deck – and quietly.
- No fighting allowed on board. All arguments were to be settled on land under the supervision of the quartermaster. The rivals were first asked to fight a duel with pistols but if they both missed, it was out with the old swords. The winner was the first to draw blood.
- No gambling or women were allowed on board. Women prisoners were protected by armed guards.

On one occasion, when mildly insulted by a drunken crew member, Roberts ran the poor guy through with his sword, on the spot. Someone else in the crew, a chap called Jones, yet another Welshman (what is it about the Welsh and piracy?), thought this a bit over the top and had the nerve to curse the captain and attack him, throwing him clean over a cannon. A mini mutiny looked imminent but at the quartermaster's quickly convened inquiry, it was decided that for the whole business to work (being pirates and all), the captain must at all times be respected and obeyed, and that Jones should have two lashes of the cat-o'-nine-tails from each member of the crew. This normally wouldn't have been so bad, but at that time there were 180 of 'em.

On another occasion in 1722, when one of eleven English slave ships failed to surrender, Robert's crew poured tar over the deck and set fire to the ship with eighty of the poor chaps on board, still chained together in pairs. This created a bit of a dilemma — either leap over the side and be lunch (double portion) for the sharks that were milling around in the surrounding waters, or stay to be roasted alive. Tricky eh!

Black Bart and his sixty crew were to become legendary throughout the Caribbean and around the African coast for their sheer nerve and stupendous sailing ability, at times attacking up to twenty-six ships in one go.

Vendetta

Roberts had a right thing about sailors from either of the islands of Martinique or Barbados because of their Governor's constant and annoying attempts to catch him. If he ever captured any, he would either cat-o'-nine-tail them almost to a pulp, cut off their ears, or tie them to the main mast and use them for target practice. (Not their ears — the sailors!) Once, when capturing a ship sailing out of Martinique, Roberts discovered to his great glee that she was carrying the island's Governor. Black Bart thought it a great laugh to have him hanged from the yardarm and left dangling there for the rest of the trip.

Roberts died as he had lived, attacking a far stronger naval vessel, the *Swallow*, that had been trying for eight months to catch him. The brave buccaneer, not yet forty, had his throat ripped open by some stray grapeshot. His crew were instantly broken and disillusioned without him (some even cried out loud — big sissies) and were soon captured. Actually it was later revealed that most of them were still drunk from the merriment of the night before and couldn't have fought to save their miserable lives. Many of those captured, unfortunately (depending on which way you look at it), died on their way to trial, but it would hardly have done them any good if they hadn't, for, all in all, fifty-two were hanged and eighteen of the very naughtiest were cut down, tarred and hung in cages from gibbets till they eventually rotted right down to their bare bones.

Edward (Ned) Low – The Cruellest

Another brilliant mariner, Edward Low, was a Londoner, born in Westminster at the beginning of the eighteenth century. As a lad he couldn't read or write and made a living by stealing coins off other boys and beating them up if they objected. He emigrated, when young, to Boston in America, and began work as a ship rigger (the only honest thing he ever did) before going to sea in 1721. Low soon fell out with his first captain, and even fired off a shot at him. Luckily it missed but unluckily it blew the brains out of another crew member who was rather carelessly standing behind him.

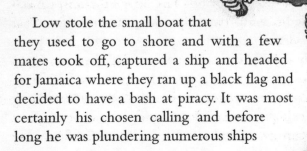

WHOOPS - SORRY!

Low stole the small boat that they used to go to shore and with a few mates took off, captured a ship and headed for Jamaica where they ran up a black flag and decided to have a bash at piracy. It was most certainly his chosen calling and before long he was plundering numerous ships and having a high old time in, out and around about the Caribbean. But all this was kids' stuff and Low eventually captured a magnificent schooner that he fancied as his main boat and appropriately called her the *Fancy*. He then took on loads more men and went pirating in earnest.

His reputation grew within only a year, not only for the boats he robbed, but for the enormous cruelty he used while doing it. The stories of his barbarity are legendary, especially against the Spaniards and French whom he hated. At one time he overtook a Spanish privateer and on examination discovered they had taken prisoner a group of captains from recently overhauled American ships. Now Low wasn't wild about Yanks at the best of times, but at least they weren't Spanish. On the basis of the old pirate saying – 'dead men tell no tales' – he promptly slaughtered everyone aboard and any that went over the side in terror were relentlessly pursued in boats and clubbed senseless as they tried to swim for safety. He then burned the ship and sank her.

'Admiral' Low (as he eventually called himself) wasn't keen on the Portuguese either. He once took a Portuguese ship on its way home from Brazil with a fortune in gold on board. Well, not actually on board; the captain had hung the coins in a large sack outside his cabin window, and when he saw the pirate ship bearing down on him, he cut it loose and let it sink to the bottom of the ocean (where it presumably still is). For this Mr Low cut off the captain's lips, boiled them in oil and then murdered his thirty-two shipmates in front of him. That must really re-define 'angry'.

At the end of his career, as he was on the run from HMS *Greyhound*, he became so furious at her persistence that he decided to take it out on anyone he came across. First along was a large whaling sloop and for no good reason, he stripped the poor captain naked and cut off his ears before shooting

him through the head (at least he couldn't hear the bang!).
Then, again for no reason, he sent the poor crew off in a little
whaling boat with nothing more than a couple of dry biscuits,
some water and a compass. But worse was still to come. A day
or so later, he took the captains of two more whaling boats on
board his ship. He disembowelled one of them, then took out
his heart, cooked it and forced one of his crew to eat it. The

other one was cut
about mercilessly,
before being made to
eat his own ears, which
had been roasted but
luckily sprinkled
with salt and pepper
(unfortunately
ketchup hadn't been
invented). There's
no record of the

poor unfortunate not enjoying the meal but they do say he
died later of his injuries.

Eventually Low was set upon by his crew for murdering
the quartermaster in his sleep after a tiff, and was put
overboard with a couple of his mates in a little boat with no
provisions. Their luck was in – well sort of. They were picked
up by a ship shortly afterwards. But it was a French ship (the
French were after Ned Low and Co. even more than anyone
else) and they threw him and his mates in irons and took them
off to the French island of Martinique, where they were tried
and then hanged for crimes against humanity. Or were they?
Some historians tell another story – that Low escaped and
disappeared off the face of the earth.

Henry Morgan – The Most Successful

Yet *another* Welshman (I give up), Henry Morgan, was born in 1635 into a well-to-do military family. Henry wanted to be a soldier, and joined the expeditionary force of 7,000 troops sent to capture the Spanish stronghold of Hispaniola. When that didn't work, the two commanders turned about and decided to have a go at Jamaica which turned out to be a doddle.

CAPTAIN MORGAN

Gradually Morgan got to lead his own raids on Jamaica and he gained great fame as one of the most fierce and feared enemies of the Spanish. When Edward Mansfield, the leader of the privateers (respectable pirates), was executed by the Spaniards, Morgan was chosen to replace him and at only thirty-two he became 'Admiral of the Brethren of the Coas', a wily band of buccaneers and ill-disguised cut-throat pirates. Their greatest coup was to capture the Spanish stronghold and largest port in South America, Porto Bello (or Puerto Bello, in foreign), against ridiculous odds. He then sent a cheeky letter to the President of Panama saying he could have his town back for 350,000 pesos (rather a lot), or Morgan would burn the place to the ground. After much to-ing and fro-ing, Morgan walked (or sailed) away with a cool £250,000 in gold coins, silver bars and chests chock-full of silver plate. Everyone back home in England was over the moon and Morgan was an overnight superhero. But by now our Henry had got the taste for money and was soon out a-plundering once more.

Got a Light?

After one such raid Morgan and the lads celebrated so hard and became so drunk that someone accidentally dropped a lighted something or other near the gunpowder supply and the whole ship was blown to smithereens. Our Henry, lucky as ever, was picked up in the sea, a trifle damp but otherwise OK – one of only ten survivors.

Captain Henry Morgan went on to wreak more havoc amongst the Spanish, but as he did so he gained a reputation for cruelty far beyond what was necessary. His destruction of the city of Panama went down in history as an orgy of looting, killing and torture that has seldom been equalled. More to the point, many of his attacks occurred after a peace treaty had already been signed between England and Spain, which naturally got him into deep trouble. Also, he was terribly unfair when it came to sharing out the spoils with his crew, always taking the lion's share for himself.

Despite all this, the admittedly brave captain still had a charmed life and was knighted in 1674 and sent back to Jamaica as its Lieutenant Governor. The ultimate joke was that in the following years, until his death in 1668, the fabulously wealthy Sir Henry Morgan spent most of his time suppressing buccanneering and piracy, hanging hundreds of his former mates and associates, which was a bit ironic – not to mention two-faced – when you come to think of it.

God Speaks?

In 1692, Port Royal, reputedly the most wicked town in the Western hemisphere, was destroyed by a massive earthquake, burying for ever the tomb of the notorious and illustrious Henry Morgan.

'Gentleman' Stede Bonnet – The Poshest

Major Stede Bonnet was different from all the other pirates and buccaneers. Born in 1688, he became a respected, educated and extremely cultured man of letters and went into piracy merely to get away from his missus whose nagging was driving him round the bend (or out to sea). Bonnet had owned a substantial sugar plantation on the island of Barbados until, suddenly, without warning, and knowing about as much as you or I do about the sea (sorry if you're an expert), disappeared. Secretly, he'd fitted out a fast sloop, which he called the *Revenge*, with ten guns and an extensive library of his favourite books, had assembled a crew of seventy similarly minded men and then simply sailed off into the sunset to look for fame and fortune – brilliant stuff! And wasn't he good at it. After lots of fun on the high seas, he eventually ended up in the same flotilla as Blackbeard, with his ship the *Revenge* (now sporting thirty guns and a crew of 300) and becoming, like Edward Teach, a big name in the world of piracy. The debonair major, by the way, was often to be seen, taking no part in the actual sailing, but strolling about on deck in a silk morning gown, drink in one hand and one of his many volumes in the other.

Later on, a contrite Bonnet managed to sweet-talk his way into a pardon for his dastardly deeds, and was even given a privateer's commission to act against the Spanish (he could now rob, murder and pillage legally). But the miffed major had a few old scores to settle with Blackbeard, who'd cheated him out of a large share of the loot, so, instead of going after the Spanish, like he'd promised, he set out in the opposite direction to chase the old dog down. He soon forgot all about privateering and, changing his name to Captain Roberts and the sloop's to the *Royal James*, set about robbing and looting with new passion.

Bonnet (alias Roberts) was eventually captured after a long, bloodthirsty and spectacular chase and he and his men were brought to Charles Town for trial. But Charles Town had no gaol and Bonnet and his men were kept in the watch-house . . . but not very well. Bonnet and his sailing master escaped that night and the major soon had the unheard of sum of £700 on his aristocratic head.

But they were quickly recaptured and at his trial the judge really let him have it for committing eleven acts of piracy after he'd been pardoned, and killing eighteen naval men who'd been sent to get him. Bonnet was apparently gobsmacked at the death sentence and was taken grovelling, posy in hand, and making an awful fuss, to be hanged with the rest of his men at a special gallows in Charleston Harbour.

IT WASN'T ME.
HONEST!

Francis L'Olonnois – The All-Round Nastiest

There's bad pirates, there's very bad pirates and then, way out in front in the badness stakes there's Francis L'Olonnois. Born Jean David Nau, at the back end of the seventeenth century, he started life as a lowly bonded servant on one of the West Indian islands before moving to the pirate island of Hispaniola. He then became one of the boucaniers (no, I haven't spelt it wrong, they were forest hunters and meat curers described on page 9). Then he joined with others to start proper buccaneering, first from canoes and then from small ships which they captured. The young Frenchman was noted for his almost lunatic courage and was soon given a commission to have a proper go at the big Spanish treasure ships.

After many hair-raising adventures he was eventually reported dead to the Governor of Cuba. But the wily old Governor didn't believe it and sent a posse of ships to track him down which they eventually did.

But it all went very pear-shaped and ended up with L'Ollonois, on board the ship that had been attacking him, personally chopping off the heads, one by one, of all those who'd hidden below decks, as they poked their heads out to see what was going on. All save one, who was spared simply so he could report back to the Governor.

The vicious pirate's small armada gradually grew to eight separate ships with 700 men, and together they robbed and plundered and murdered right down as far as Mexico and Nicaragua, looting small coastal cities to the tune of 260,000 pieces of eight. The stories of their cruel and unrelenting torture almost defy belief, with L'Ollonois in the thick of it, literally, on some occasions, licking with great relish, the blood from his hard-worked sword.

Just as an example, on one occasion, when a prisoner

claimed he did not know a route to his home town that our Francis was trying to reach and plunder, the monster ripped him open, tore out his heart, chewed on it and then threw it in the face of his friend saying that he'd do the same to him if he didn't play ball.

Eventually, by poetic justice, L'Ollonois himself was captured by a band of grumpy Indians, who took great delight in hacking him limb from limb, cooking him in a big pot and then eating him for supper.

Rahmah Ibn Jabir – The Craziest

Rahmah Ibn Jabir was a tribal leader and the most feared pirate in the Persian Gulf until he died in 1826. He was famed for never bothering with prisoners, slaughtering every member of the crew of the countless vessels he overran. Oddly enough he never attacked British ships as he hoped they would one day help him against his Arab foes (which they didn't). He is also remembered for the shocking physical state he had managed to get himself into through his awful antics. Here's a report from a British captain J.S. Buckingham:

> Cut and hacked, and pierced with wounds of sabres, spears and bullets, in every part [every part!!] . . . He had, besides, a face naturally ferocious and ugly, and rendered still more so with several scars there, and by the loss of one eye. This Butcher Chief, who is said to have 200 wives, affects great simplicity in garb and manners . . . His usual dress is a shirt which is never taken off until it is worn out, no drawers [chilly or what?] or covering for the legs, a large black goatskin wrapped over all, and a close-fitting handkerchief on his head.

But that was nothing. Apparently a gun-blast had smashed his left arm to the point that there was no bone between the elbow and shoulder and the arm simply hung on withered skin and tendons wrapped round with silver wire.

He died at seventy, blind as a bat and reduced to one ship (he once had a large fleet). But even then old Rahmah went out in style. Holding his youngest son, aged eight, aloft, he tossed a burning spar into a barrel of gunpowder*, blowing himself, the lad, his own ship and the ship that had been trying to capture him, to smithereens and then to the bottom of the deep blue sea.

---

* *Difficult with one arm, I'd have thought!*

HANGING AROUND
AT WAPPING

If piracy had become your chosen profession, it was generally regarded as a bad idea to get caught. Then as now, any kind of naughtiness on the high seas was likely to make the powers-that-be (or were) very cross indeed. In the pirates' and mutineers' cases the trial was generally an open and shut one – no warnings, reprimands or light fines etc. The penalty, death – by hanging – and in public – was almost inevitable. London was a favourite venue for hanging, particularly Wapping – a murky, smelly, labyrinth of docks, gin shops, wharves, alehouses, brothels and boat builders, all crammed together in a tangle of rope-strewn masts (now a tangle of city brokers with mobile phones).

Between Wapping New Stairs and King Henry's Stairs, as they are called today, was the notorious Execution Dock, a gallows designed purely for punishing pirates. These unfortunates were destined to 'dance the hempen jig', as some wit called it, on a rope just above the waterline at low tide. There they would be hanged pathetically just above the oozing mud, as the filthy Thames covered their limp bodies for three tides – a symbol of the jurisdiction of the Lord High Admiral. He was the guy whose job it was to oversee the punishment of all those who did their dirty deeds on the high seas and waterways up to low tide mark. Crimes committed above the tide mark were tried by the civil courts. On the other side of the river, built on piles, was (and still is) the ancient Angel Inn, where that old tyrant Judge Jeffreys (the hanging judge) would sit having a quiet drink while watching his condemned subjects being 'turned off' as he so charmingly put it, across the water (beats darts, I suppose).

Up till 1723 only the captain and the quartermaster of a pirate ship would have actually been hanged, but the war against piracy became so frenzied that it was decided to string up anyone who'd even sniffed a pirate boat, let alone sailed under the Jolly Roger. Except, of course, for those who'd been captured at sea and forced into it. Needless to say, the most common defence of your average accused pirate was that he had been made to sign the pirates' articles (and who can blame him), but they seldom got away with it as they were usually shopped by the ones who'd already been told they were going to swing. Others swore blind that they knew the whereabouts of lots of other pirates and would help track them down if their lives were spared. There really is no honour amongst thieves or pirates.

THICK AS
A
PIRATE
↓

Execution Day

An execution was a fun day out for all of the average London family in the sixteenth and seventeenth centuries, and the demise of a dastardly pirate was probably the best gig of all. Hours before it happened, crowds would arrive at Execution Dock from both sides of the river – at that time it was relatively easy to cross by horse and cart at low tide. Not only that, but boats would sail up river and down river (at high tide) to moor near the gallows in order to get the best view possible. Such a laugh!

Eventually the dismal procession would arrive from either the Newgate or Marshalsea prisons, led by the Admiral Marshal carrying a silver oar (to prove his authority). The pirate or pirates in question would be manacled in a heavily guarded cart, and they would sometimes chink their chains cheekily to the throng of leering Londoners who would hurl the most obscene abuse (and worse!) as they passed. It was a tradition for pirates to die with as much bravado as possible, so they would often dress in their finest clothes, festooned in red and blue ribbons. One even kicked his footwear into the crowd, joking that he could never be seen to die with his shoes on.

The gibbet at Hanging Dock was a relatively simple affair – just two vertical posts and a cross member from which the rope or ropes would dangle. The pirate would be asked (not very nicely) to climb up a shortish ladder where a noose would be put over his head. All the executioner had to do was pull the ladder away. Money for old rope! In those days hanging did not always kill the customer immediately, especially if their neck didn't break at first drop, so it was quite common for relatives to swing on their nearest and dearest's legs to hasten his horrible end – a grisly sight, but just what the audience ordered. After the three tides had washed over them, the buccaneers' bodies would either be chucked into unmarked graves or hung up again in special cages that were positioned along various parts of the river, till they rotted to their bare bones – a warning to any other ordinary sailors who thought they might fancy a bit of light piracy.

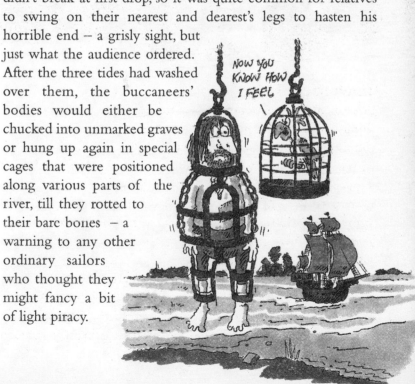

The Kidd Gets it

In 1701 the body of the notorious villain Captain William Kidd, who'd been kept for a year in the hideous Newgate Prison, was hung on a special gibbet at Tilbury Point in a terrifying harness of iron hoops and chains, so that mariners could observe his rotting, crow-pecked corpse for more than an hour as they swept round that wide and desolate part of the Thames. Even more eerie, he'd been painted black all over, with the same tar that they'd coat the bottoms of the ships with, just so that he'd last that bit longer. (Please don't try this on the dog.)

The cage was constructed of strong iron, firstly so that relatives couldn't steal the body to give it a decent burial and secondly so that the skeleton could be held in place once the flesh had rotted or been pecked away by those peckish crows.

Across the Atlantic and around the Caribbean it was a similar deal. Convicted pirates would dangle on special gibbets planted on the little outcrops that poked above the water at the approaches to those Caribbean islands that the pirates had terrorised for so long. On the Eastern coast of America, around Charleston, South Carolina, or Newport, Rhode Island and particularly Boston, justice was short and swift, pirates being hung out like bunting at a fairground.

Sometimes if the pirates knew that there was no escaping the rope, they went out fighting in great style. On one occasion in 1720 a pirate awaiting his death in Virginia, demanded a bottle of wine and, as he swigged a glass, 'Drank Damnation to the Governor and Confusion to the Colony.

In England between 1716 and 1726, over 400 convicted

pirates were executed, and the rest went to a fate that some thought even worse – the dreaded hulks – those decommissioned, clapped-out sloops and galleons that were moored in the vast lonely estuary of the Thames and used as prisons.

French Treat

Captured French corsairs (commissioned pirates) were often sent to these miserable Thames hulks (*pontons* in your actual French) where they were treated even more appallingly (we never did have much time for the French, at the best of times). One such prisoner was recorded as saying in 1797, 'For the last eight weeks we have been reduced to eating dogs, cats and rats ... the only rations we get consist of mouldy bread ... rotten meat, and brackish water'. That's rich, I reckon, coming from a country that gobbles up snails and the back legs off frogs at the drop of a *chapeau*, but we won't go into that now!

Forgotten

Spanish Pirate Antonio Mendoza had it even worse. The authorities of St Christopher's colony cut off his ears, burned out his tongue with a red-hot iron and left him literally to rot in a forgotten dungeon.

Unlike today, from around the middle of the eighteenth century pirates weren't regarded in the least bit as heroes by the general public – for anyone who had to travel on the high seas would have been at their mercy. They were generally regarded by all and sundry as enemies of all mankind, and it must be said that the relentless and savage hangings certainly acted as a deterrent to anyone contemplating answering a pirate ad down the local job centre.

Time Scale

Although the golden age for pirates was only really between the mid-seventeenth and the early eighteenth centuries, the very first hanging for robbery on the high seas was in 1228 and the very last as recently as 1840.

THE END OF THE VOYAGE

The Golden Age of the pirate came to a speedy finale in the early nineteenth century when a massive $500,000 was set aside to create a special crack squadron under American Commodore David Porter. He put together eight super-fast schooners, a new-fangled steam-powered warship and five flat-bottomed landing craft to attack the buccaneers when ashore. Last and most brilliant of all, he added the ultimate sitting duck – a ship that looked just like a ponderous old merchant vessel, but packed six massive cannon. With a gang of 1,500 tough marines, this little armada joined the six hard-worked US warships that were already in the Caribbean searching for the bewildered buccaneers. In a couple of years the game was up, hundreds of pirates were captured or killed and the rest simply disappeared into thin air.

One of the very last acts of piracy in the Atlantic Ocean took place on 20th September 1832, when the pirate ship *Panda* intercepted an American brig the *Mexican*, which just happened to be carrying $20,000 worth of silver bars to Argentina from Salem on the north east coast of America. When the pirates politely asked their captain, a nasty bit of work called Pedro Gilbert, what to do with the captives, he replied rather oddly, 'dead cats don't mew, you know what to do' – obviously a feline version of the old pirate saying 'dead men tell no tales'. The pirate crew promptly relieved the ship of its silver, ordered the crew downstairs, chucked in a load of oil-soaked rags, battened down the hatches and set fire to what they planned would become the poor innocents' floating coffin. The crew luckily broke out, but cleverly kept the fire going until the pirate ship was over the horizon (just in case they came back). A few months later, Gilbert and Co.

were caught loading slaves on the African coast by a British warship which took them straightaway to Boston and hanged 'em.

But that was then and now is now. Piracy, I have to report, is back, and with a vengeance. Not as it was in the past – ragged brigands in romantic sailing ships, armed with cutlasses, muskets and cannons and stuff; but highly professional criminals in high-speed cruisers, armed to the teeth with Kalashnikovs and rocket launchers, careering around the Indian Ocean and the South China Seas, hijacking cargo boats and private yachts for all they're worth – not a parrot or a wooden leg in sight. Likewise, the prizes are also different – no Spanish gold or Aztec jewellery these days. According to Interpol (international police) modern pirates go after stuff they can shift easily; boring stuff like paint, rope and household commodities. But they are just as ruthless, often tying up the crew and leaving them on board their ship while it ploughs ahead through busy, congested waters. As a defence against this new surge in maritime naughtiness a Piracy Centre was set up in 1992 in Malaysia where owners and captains alike can ring up to report anything suspicious.

But it's a bit like trying to turn back the very sea they sail in. Piracy and pirates, whatever colour or creed, are here to stay and very little can be done to stop them. Wherever there is a defenceless vessel bobbing around on a big, lonely ocean, there will always be those who think it might be a laugh to teach them a lesson they'll never forget. I don't know about you, but when it comes right down to it, I think that, if we'd never had pirates I, for one, would jolly well miss 'em.